COLLEGEVILLE

COLLEGEVILLE

To [name],

Enjoy

Mk Sipe

A PHOTO ESSAY · MIKE & MICHAEL SIPE

HISTORY · HILARY THIMMESH O.S.B.

in memory of

JOE O'CONNELL: 1927–1995

PAUL SCHWIETZ, O.S.B.: 1952–2000

The influence that Collegeville has had on me has stretched over nearly fifty years. When I was just a child it was the mystique of a faraway place that transformed boys into priests. I remember being in second grade at Sacred Heart grade school in Robbinsdale, Minnesota, when Sister Mariom presented me with a full wardrobe of doll-size vestments that were perfect replicas of the real thing. She said I should have the vestments because of the honor of having a brother who was becoming a priest at Saint John's in Collegeville.

We made the long trip to Collegeville many times during those thirteen years (1946 to 1959) before my brother Dick was ordained. Some of my earliest memories were of my sister Liz and I getting carsick in the Big I, a 1952 Chrysler Imperial. My dad would smoke a cigar or chew snuff. If you were sitting in the back seat you needed to duck when Dad opened the window at 60 miles an hour to spit. And of course we were *always* sitting in the back seat. But Liz found a way to finagle her way to the front seat every once in awhile.

When we arrived at Collegeville we drove deep into the woods before reaching the impressive twin towers of the old Abbey Church. We would visit Dick in a small room just off the main entrance down from the old church entrance. During those visits I mostly sat and wondered. I wondered what Saint John's was like. What was behind the doors, especially the ones labeled PRIVATE MONASTIC AREA? I thought maybe I would be a priest, but that thought never lasted long. Mainly I thought about how different this place seemed compared to any other place I had ever seen. Of course I was only about eight at the time and hadn't seen much.

In 1960, ready for high school and wanting to follow three of my older brothers, it was my turn to go to Saint John's Prep School in Collegeville. I spent the next eight years there (including four years attending Saint John's University). I lived two years in the old open dorms on the top floor of one of the first buildings in Collegeville—affectionately known as the Quad. I finished out prep school at what seemed the luxurious—albeit concrete—semi-open dorms at the new prep school. These were built with the same flair as the new Abbey Church that was designed by the famous architect, Marcel Breuer, and completed in 1961.

The Breuer buildings are a stark contrast to the old brick buildings. During my time on campus, the church, prep school, library, science hall, and two university dorms were all built with the Breuer touch. Also during those years, I witnessed the beginning of the football dynasty led by coach John Gagliardi, who now holds the all-time record for the most wins of any college coach. I was at Saint John's when the team won national titles in 1963 and 1965. I graduated in 1968 with a BS in economics and accounting.

Although I saw many changes at Collegeville between 1960 and 1968, I didn't notice the beauty of the place then! My avocation as a photographer was just budding at the time. As my photography interest has grown, I've been much more attracted to the aesthetics of Collegeville. In the '60s I was preoccupied with sports, classes, the war, and Bennies (the affectionate term for the women of our sister school, the College of Saint Benedict). In 1967 I married my wife of 37 years, Patty. I became particularly interested in the harmony of the landscape, structures, and people of Collegeville during the eight years our children, Bridget and Michael, were attending Saint John's Prep School and University and the College of Saint Benedict.

ABOUT THE BOOK

This project began in the mid-1980s as a beautiful and familiar place for me to practice my photography passion. Then in 1992 after Michael graduated from SJU with a BA in German and Sociology, he decided to pursue professional photography. He asked if he could work with me on the Collegeville Project. Of course, I was delighted. Since then the satisfying images have increased to the point where we are now able to share them. As we took more and more pictures, little did I know that the result would be a photo essay on the avocations of the people of Collegeville—farmers, sculptors, painters, potters, gardeners, musicians, coaches, athletes, educators, worshipers, and of course, photographers.

We have no intention of creating a complete and accurate photo documentary of Collegeville. Our intent has always been to capture on film what we think is artistic. Consequently, in addition to a visualization of the many avocations, we have images of a number of landscapes and two buildings in particular—the Abbey Church (six images) and the Quadrangle (six images). The hope is that this composite of our work illustrates the natural and constructed beauty of Collegeville and its residents.

With few words and little contact, one Collegeville resident, Joe O'Connell, inspired Michael and me to dedicate this book to him and to contribute half of the profits to the scholarship fund for art students in his name. Joe was a resident artist at the College of Saint Benedict for forty years. Three months prior to his death from cancer, as he was struggling to finish his limestone sculptures for Christ the King Catholic Community in Las Vegas, he allowed us to photograph him not once but twice. Twice, because the 4 x 5 camera was not the best choice for this very important environmental portrait; we needed to come back with a 6 x 17 panoramic camera and take the photo in black-and-white.

The other half of the profits from the book will be contributed to the Saint John's Arboretum in the name of its founding director, Paul Schwietz, O.S.B., who died May 4, 2000 just three years after realizing his dream, when the lands he worked so hard to preserve and restore were dedicated as an arboretum.

Michael was responsible for virtually all the environmental portraits. When I look at his professional portfolio this is clearly one of his strengths. Look closely at Joe O'Connell (pages 98 and 99), Monks in front of Garden House (page 105), Brother Placid and white horse (page 103) and Father Gall (page 95). These are phenomenal photographs. That being said, my favorite image is still the Quad roof (page 115). Michael captured this image standing precariously on a radiator (with the assistance of my steady hand holding the tripod positioned dangerously on the radiator) looking through a partially fogged window on a rainy fall football Saturday.

ABOUT THE PHOTOGRAPHS

Many of the images in this book were captured with a Wisner 4 x 5 large-format field camera. The panoramas were taken with a Fuji G6 x 17. Other cameras used included a Wisner 8 x 10, Mamiya 6 x 7, Pentax 6 x 7, Bronica 2-1/4, and a Nikon F3 35mm. The film was not as varied.

The color film was primarily Fuji Velvia; the black-and-white, Kodak Tri X. Exposure times were a fraction of a second to two minutes (for the interior of Collegeville Orchard store page 55). Notice the faint image of Jody O'Connell in the window of their charming entryway (page 101) as she came and left during a 60-second exposure.

The only filtration that was used was for color correction (5 or 10 magenta) on long exposures and warming filters (81a and 81b) when the sun was a little high or on a cloudy day. The 5 magenta became an addiction and may have been used a little beyond just correction. In

fact, I often wear rose-color glasses because I like the tint in my little view of the world.

Images were taken in color only if color had an impact. Otherwise, black-and-white was used. In some cases, black-and-white was essential to attain the desired effect. Consequently, in a single publication we have an uncommon combination of formats depicting an uncommon place.

MIKE SIPE

A quiet paved country road meandering its way through miniature hills and valleys, farms and houses that are always perfectly silent when I have passed by. The old train tracks that served as the backbone to Collegeville are gone. But the simple oversized black-and-white Collegeville sign stands purposefully. "Slow down and be deliberate in your efforts" is now what I see on that sign.

This project, much like the image of the maple tree with bags (page 83) has involved us in a slow process of wandering and being open to what we find and what we follow. Over the years I have walked out to the old chapel many times, finding along the way familiar memories stored in bridges and rocks, trees and statues. How precious these keepers are for us; how powerful a bend in the road is. With each new hike in the woods I find new inspirations to explore and to continue the connections made decades earlier

Dad began this project "officially" in 1985 when he received his Wisner 4 x 5 field camera. Soon after, I began assisting him. The box camera and my father's slow methodical technique both captivated and frustrated me. When I would go out with him in the early years of this project, as is true now we would always collaborate on the vision/scene. His eye for landscapes has always been more evolved than mine. He composed with ease most of the landscapes in this book and whatever changes I made to some of these beautiful compositions were minor if anything.

Once the crop was set and I had unwrapped the obligatory 10 magenta filter then the long painful wait would begin (that was the subject of more than a few disagreements, I taking a purist approach to photographing nature, not yet understanding the concept of reciprocity failure). Once my father had his spot meter in hand, I would have just enough time to build a small lean-to, get a fire going, and cook up a string of perch from the lake. What I understand now that I only vaguely did then was that he would be able to capture the image in one or maybe two sheets of film, which in itself speaks volumes. Some of the last landscapes he made for this book were actually captured on the fly as the last rays of the day unfolded an exotic tongue across late autumn fields (page 58). Deliberate technique has no place in these moments. These seemingly fleeting landscapes invite without time to consider. They are spirited events that pour themselves out to those who are open and aware.

The land, people, and history are the spirit of Collegeville. Incomplete as it will always be in both words and pictures, this book represents a continued effort to create in much the same tradition that built Saint John's and the greater Collegeville community. It gives thanks to what has come before us, engages us to learn and create, and involves us in the human experience. Enjoy.

MICHAEL SIPE

THE EARLY YEARS

It wasn't Collegeville to begin with. It was St. Louis on the Lake.

Five Benedictine monks came out to the Minnesota Territory from Pennsylvania in 1856 to serve the German Catholic settlers in the region. They stopped at St. Paul, then came up the river to St. Cloud. After a few years they moved from there to a farm they had cleared in a "beautiful valley"—Schoenthal—near the eventual site of Collegeville station; in later years they would call it the "Old Farm." In 1866 they settled at their permanent location on the shores of Lake Sagatagan, gained the status of an abbey called St. Louis on the Lake, and elected their first abbot, Rupert Seidenbusch.

The abbey developed rapidly. To power a gristmill and a sawmill, the monks dammed a stream on the west side of their farmyard, thus creating the picturesque Watab (or Stump) Lake meandering between their land and Civil War veteran Peter Eich's farmstead. It was an age that valued the picturesque. In 1872, across Lake Sagatagan at a vantage point overlooking the water, some of the young monks built a small chapel with a white steeple and dedicated it to Mary, Star of the Sea. Rebuilt and repaired from time to time, it still stands there welcoming hikers and having its picture taken.

The monks built a brickyard and started putting up brick buildings. By 1874 a south wing, a main building, and a north wing, constructed in that sequence, housed the monastery and the school, and presented an impressive east front looking out on a field of stumps where the boys played games in good weather. Sheds and barns—including a brick butcher shop and a smokehouse that still stand—dotted the farmyard behind it.

Abbot Rupert became Bishop Seidenbusch and moved to St. Cloud in 1875. The monks now numbered 55 priests, lay brothers, and juniors. The school, called Saint John's College, was organized on a European model with a junior course, a classical course, and a theological course, all of them together enrolling 130 students when Alexius Edelbrock became the second abbot in 1875.

Abbot Alexius was 33 years old and a son of the frontier with the self-confidence of an empire builder. He changed the name of the abbey to Saint John's, added a commercial course to the college, started missions to the Ojibwa Indians at White Earth and Red Lake, and started the Industrial School for Indian boys at Saint John's. He reached as far afield as northern Minnesota and North Dakota to found parishes, schools, and hospitals in cooperation with the Benedictine sisters in St. Joseph.

THE BEGINNINGS OF COLLEGEVILLE

Collegeville began in 1879. That was the year when the St. Paul and Pacific Railroad—later the Great Northern—built a station with a post office where its tracks angled through the Old Farm a mile or so northeast of the monastery and called it Collegeville. Henry Broker, the first station agent and postmaster, also operated a small general store out of his new house on the north side of the tracks. His descendants, both Brokers and Wittrocks, remain property owners in the area to this day.

Conrad Diekmann was appointed postmaster in 1923 and was in turn succeeded by his daughter Marie in 1929. Two of the Diekmann boys, Conrad and Leo, became monks, Conrad and Godfrey. Gradually a small colony of residents connected with Saint John's grew up around the station and along

the road to the abbey. Among them were Emerson and Arleen Hynes at "Kilfenora," and Joseph (Joe) and Jody O'Connell on a site that turned into a corner lot when construction of I-94 in 1977 resulted in leveling the north half of their lawn for a frontage road. Joe commented on this development in his engraving, "Thou Shall not Try to Stop that which We Know to be Progress."

In time, Saint John's and Collegeville became synonymous. The postal facilities were moved to the campus in 1955. More recently the train tracks were removed and the railroad right-of-way became part of the Lake Wobegon Trail.

THE ABBEY EXPANDS

At the same time that Collegeville got its name, Abbot Alexius addressed primitive living conditions at the abbey. The fine new buildings had no central heating, not much plumbing, and no lighting other than lamps and candles. He added major new buildings. A church, attached to the north wing, was completed in 1882. In the next four years he more than doubled the space under one roof by extending the main building and the church and connecting them with a west wing to form a quadrangle. Some of the monks thought he lacked a spiritual outlook. He resigned under pressure in 1889, but not before he saw a powerhouse completed to provide steam heat through what the abbey chronicler called "an enormous net-work of pipes."

The next year a brick water tower with a castellated roofline imitating a medieval keep was erected on the highest point of ground east of the buildings. It is still there, though now hidden in the woods across the road from the Prep School. It is still in use as a reservoir for the ground watering system.

There were no trees around the water tower when it was new. The professor of astronomy, Peter Engel, thus had an uninterrupted view of the sky from his improvised observatory on the water tower roof. Four years later when he became abbot, a proper brick observatory with firm foundations and a revolving dome was built. There was a fine monastic solidity about this charming little Palomar but it didn't stand quite long enough to be appreciated as a historic building. It was demolished to make room for the new Prep School buildings in 1961.

Peter Engel was abbot from the end of 1894 until his death in 1921. He came into office five months after the abbey barely escaped destruction by a tornado that swept in over the lake toward 9 o'clock on a late June evening, brushed the top floor off the south wing, removed the chimneys from the rest of the Quad, and left the farm buildings—including a splendid new brick barn—in shambles. No one was hurt, but the disaster was generally thought to have hastened the death of Abbot Bernard Locnikar, the successor of Alexius Edelbrock. The avenue of Norway spruce in the monastery garden is part of the planting that took place in the aftermath of the storm.

Under the direction of Peter Engel and his successor Alcuin Deutsch, Saint John's Abbey was in strong and steady hands for 55 years. Alcuin resigned in 1950 and died a year later. Although their temperaments were quite different, Peter *gemuetlich*, Alcuin peremptory, both were sturdy monks and disciplined scholars.

They were surrounded by men of the same mold. Alexius Hoffmann was one of them. He was the librarian for many years, kept a copious journal, and wrote the purple-bound *Saint John's University: 1857-1907*, a year-by-year chronology that is still good reading. The three-story library building (now Wimmer Hall) constructed in 1901 had a photo studio on the third floor where Abbot Peter and Fridolin Tembreull produced many of the thousands of glass negatives now in the archives.

Oswald Baran headed a small group of monks from Saint John's sent west in 1895 to found St. Martin's monastery at Lacey, Washington. William Baldus, one of the group, returned to Saint John's to be cook and baker of the distinctive loaf that eventually became famous as Johnny bread. Another, Philip Killian, was a Civil War veteran who learned nursing willy-nilly when his Minnesota regiment was shipped down to Helena, Arkansas, in summer 1864 and promptly contracted typhoid and malaria in large numbers. This list could be extended with many more names on the farm, in the school, and in a growing number of parishes and missions.

At home the number of students increased gradually. A football team was formed in 1900 and defeated the College of St. Thomas in 1901. By the jubilee year of 1907 there were some 300 students, 32 of them seminarians, the rest distributed in secondary and college-level courses. In addition to the library, a gymnasium was built in 1901; a convent (now St. Francis House) for the sisters—at first French Presentation, later German Franciscan—who staffed the kitchen starting in 1904; an infirmary (now Greg House, a college dorm) in 1907; the football field (now Clemens Stadium) in 1908; and a science building (now Simons Hall for the social sciences) in 1910.

Fired by enthusiasm for the new field of wireless telegraphy, Abbot Peter dedicated an 80-foot radio tower behind the science building on May 26, 1915. Unfortunately his timing was bad. On May 7 a German submarine had torpedoed the *Lusitania* with a loss of 1200 lives. In the wave of anti-German feeling that swept over the country, Saint John's was suspected of pro-German sentiment, and when America entered World War I in 1917 it was required to dismantle its radio apparatus, both sending and receiving. Saint John's radio went on the air with call letters WFBJ in 1925 after the wartime anti-German fervor had subsided.

ABBOT ALCUIN RESTRUCTURES

It was a large and relatively young community that Alcuin Deutsch was elected to head in 1921. Two young monks had died in the flu epidemic in 1917-1918, but there were 50 others aged 35 or younger, and the whole community numbered 159. Many of these were priests in parishes or missions, four of them in the Bahamas, where Chrysostom Schreiner had gone in 1891 as the forerunner of a century-long mission by Saint John's Benedictines. In Minnesota Saint John's had Indian missions on the reservations at White Earth and Red Lake, and churches in other communities as far north as Grand Portage on the Canadian border.

At home the farm continued to flourish under the direction of longtime overseer Thomas Adam. Students and monks ate a homegrown diet of corn bread and maple syrup, sausages and sauerkraut, potatoes and Johnny bread produced in the monastery's own fields and feedlots, dressed in the butcher shop, baked and cooked by the German sisters.

Abbot Alcuin inherited a building under construction. This was St. Benet's Hall, a five-story fireproof residence for college students, with a bowling alley in the basement and individual rooms so narrow that no one would think of assigning more than one student to a room—which did not prevent double occupancy from 1946 to 1996. Another structure still in use was the auditorium (1928), designed as part of a larger plan that was never realized. A solid fieldstone monastery bathhouse designed by Angelo Zankl (at the time of this writing Saint John's oldest monk at 103), and fieldstone walls for the sisters' house and the monastery garden also date from this time.

Abbot Alcuin restructured the school in 1922. It had been given the title "Saint John's University" by legislative enactment in 1883 at Abbot Alexius' urging, but its largest enrollment from year to year was at the high school level. Now the abbot separated the different levels of instruction to form a preparatory school, a college of arts and sciences, and a seminary, each with its own dean. Like his predecessors he retained the office of president.

This sorting out of academic levels made all of the parts stronger. Among the monks who held the office of dean of the college, Virgil Michel (pronounced "Michael") was the Saint John's Benedictine who brought the abbey into national prominence as a pioneer in the liturgical movement. His vision of a social order renewed in Christ by participation in a restored and vital liturgy attracted followers in the monastery and around the country. He founded the Liturgical Press and promoted Catholic social movements. He was in correspondence with Mortimer Adler about a Great Books curriculum at Saint John's when his life was cut short by an infection shortly before World War II.

The wartime draft nearly closed the college. Fourteen monks went off to war as chaplains. The air force used campus facilities for successive training sessions. Seminarians continued their studies year-round.

When the war ended, the college population rebounded. In the monastery large classes of novices—eight, ten, a dozen—appeared. The pace of community affairs quickened. In his later years as abbot, Alcuin Deutsch sent monks off to new missions in Mexico, Puerto Rico, Japan, and an interracial monastery in Kentucky. In the Bahamas he established St. Augustine's Priory. In his last months as abbot he joined in laying the cornerstone for the new diocesan seminary (now Emmaus Hall), which would displace a lovely apple orchard next to the greenhouse on the west side of the monastery garden. The building filled with 100 seminarians when it opened in 1952.

THE GLORY YEARS

The 1950s were glory years for the abbey. A new abbot, Baldwin Dworshak, was elected in the last days of 1950. The place was bursting at the seams. Nearly two hundred priests and brothers were engaged in pastoral work close to home and missions far afield. Again as many monks were at the abbey in training or

working in the shops and schools. There was an undercurrent of excitement about liturgical change in the Church, a field in which Saint John's was now a recognized leader and had a charismatic spokesman in Godfrey Diekmann. Colman Barry was writing a definitive history, *Worship and Work*, for the abbey centennial in 1956.

Abbot Baldwin was talking seriously about the need for a larger church and—egged on by liturgists and artists inside and outside of the cloister—daring to cast his thoughts on a breakthrough in ecclesiastical architecture. The result of the abbot's initiative was Marcel Breuer's hundred-year plan for the campus with a new church as the centerpiece.

What was most daring about Breuer's plan was not the unusual design of the church but the proposal to demolish most of the old buildings on the campus as new structures built in their shadows replaced them. Thus the new monastery wing jutted straight out of the front door of the main building of 1871 with a temporary link to accommodate different floor levels. As time passed, the temporary link became permanent and the shadow plan was quietly forgotten. New Breuer buildings—the church, the library, the science center, a cluster of college dorms—made some of the old buildings available for new uses. In 1979 seventeen of them were placed on the National Register of Historic Places.

Other influences, too, affected the life of the abbey. College enrollment kept pressing upward. More residence halls were built, St. Mary's for 200 students in 1951, St. Thomas Aquinas for 400 students in 1959. After 105 years of living under the same roof as the monastery, the Preparatory School moved out of the Quad and into its own classroom and dormitory buildings in 1962. The dairy herd was sold and the monks at Collegeville were no longer farmers. In 1954 the Mental Health Institute for clergy of all faiths began its twenty-year run of summer courses taught by some of the most distinguished psychiatrists in the country. Monks were free to attend and gradually absorbed

an outlook on monastic life strongly influenced by modern psychology.

A TIME OF CHANGE

Then came the '60s, Vatican II, the new Breuer church, and the Beatles. For a while Abbot Baldwin tried to persuade the monks that television had no place in the monastery. Arno Gustin, whom he had appointed as the first non-abbot president of the University in 1958, persuaded him that educational TV was a good thing. A surprising number of network shows fit that category, and "The Ed Sullivan Show," "Laugh-In," and "Candid Camera" found their way into the cloister where in an earlier generation Abbot Alcuin had banned the "silly and pernicious habit" of listening to the radio. In 1966 the monks overwhelmingly approved the funding necessary to establish Minnesota Educational Radio, now MPR.

The news from Rome in the early 1960s was exciting. Abbot Baldwin attended the ecumenical council as a participant; Godfrey Diekmann was a *peritus*. In the changed world that followed the council, far-reaching liturgical changes took place. For the monastery one such change was from Latin to English in the daily round of prayer, and from 4:45 a.m. to 7 a.m. as the starting time for a much shortened form of morning prayer. With the barrier of Latin removed, the lay brothers joined the choir, and the canonical distinction between choir monks and lay brothers was dropped.

Term abbots, women, and ecumenism were other keys to transformative changes in the abbey in the last part of the twentieth century.

The first six abbots had been elected for life. In the 1960s the rules changed and abbots were elected to serve until age sixty five or for eight years, whichever was longer. Baldwin Dworshak took advantage of this change to resign in 1971 at age sixty five after twenty strenuous years in office. His successors would have terms that were shorter though no less strenuous. For the record, the abbots since Baldwin have been: John Eidenschink (1971-1979), Jerome Theisen (1979-1992), Timothy

Kelly (1992-2000), and John Klassen (2000-present).

Women became students at Saint John's in 1956 as the seminary became a school of theology admitting women as well as men, and a few years later the all-male college combined classes with the all-female College of Saint Benedict. Where previously there had been almost no women outside of the kitchen and the laundry, women now became members of the faculty and staff. Women were fully represented among the eight or ten annual scholars at the Institute for Ecumenical and Cultural Research founded in 1967 under the leadership of Kilian McDonnell.

The ecumenical mix of Protestant and Catholic scholars at the Institute complemented the work of various monks in inter-religious dialogue and exercised a powerful influence on attitudes in the abbey. In 1983 the abbey gave the Episcopal diocese of Minnesota a 99-year rent-free lease on a parcel of land for a House of Prayer on campus. In 1999 a house was made available on a temporary basis as a monastery for Methodists. As the twentieth century drew to a close, ecumenism—perhaps even more than liturgy earlier in the century—had become a field of leadership for Saint John's.

Two events of the '80s and '90s bear witness to the ongoing relationship of the abbey to the church at large. In 1985, 1986, and 1988, the American Catholic bishops held summer meetings at Saint John's. The lack of air-conditioned dorms in the torrid summer of '88 may explain why the series ended at three, but there was a fine summer evening in 1986 when virtually the whole United States Conference of Catholic Bishops gathered for a cookout under the spreading branches of an ancient black walnut tree in the monastery garden. In an unrelated event Abbot Jerome Theisen [who had presided at Saint John's since 1979] was elected Abbot Primate, head of the Benedictine order worldwide, in 1992 and took up his duties in Rome.

SAINT JOHN'S TODAY

To bring the picture up to date, a range of other monastic developments can only be mentioned. The Saint John's monastic community got smaller as the century neared its end, partly because some of the missions matured and became independent communities, partly because monks left the community in significant numbers, partly because novitiate classes got smaller. The present size is approximately 180. Ordination to the priesthood ceased to be routine and then became exceptional. Many of the parishes were consolidated or transferred to diocesan care as monk pastors retired. Monks continued to work in the prep school, college, and school of theology but in smaller numbers and to more advanced age. A whole floor of the cloister became a retirement center staffed by health care professionals. And the monks got serious about a new building overlooking Lake Sagatagan, this time a guest house to give concrete shape to a larger and more focused guest apostolate for the future.

The pictures in this book capture the beauty and feel of the natural environment of Collegeville. They also capture the contrasting and alluring architectural design of the two dominant structures at Saint John's—the Quadrangle and the Abbey Church. But what is most amazing is the portrayal of some of the passions of the inhabitants of this remarkable community—monks and laypeople, teachers and students, Catholics and people of other faiths—as Saint John's reaches its 150th year.

HILARY THIMMESH, O.S.B

▶
CHAPEL IN THE SNOW
The Chapel of Our Lady, Star of the Sea, wears a winter mantel of
ermine under a blue sky where the moon rises for a cloudless night.

▶

ROAD ACROSS FROZEN LAKE
Pioneers hauled cords of firewood across the icebound lake on roads like
this one from the old laundry to the chapel.

▶ **BEACH CLOSED**
On a cold winter day Michael and Bridget oblige their father for the first
image taken with his new Wisner 4 x 5 camera at the beach house door.

▶

SNOWY ROAD WITH STOP SIGN
No traffic on winter's great white way. This mile-plus tree-lined
roadway was once used as the main entrance to the Saint John's campus.
Now a main artery to many paths through the largely wooded 2,500
acres of the Saint John's Arboretum.

▶

BOATS WITH FLOATS
Beached for the winter.

▶
RED CANOES
Canoes sit on the shore, ready to be released to the calm waters of
Lake Sagatagan.

▶

A SUMMER'S DAY AT THE BEACH
Norman Rockwell would have loved to paint this summer scene at the
Lake Sagatagan beach. The photographers were a few seconds late in
releasing the shutter, otherwise all three of the lifeguards would have
had ponytails.

▶
MONASTERY FLOAT IN MORNING MIST
With swimming season over, the monastery float stands empty as morning mist rises from the tranquil water.

▶

MORNING CREW
The rising sun sets the lake afire and surrounds Michael's rowing team
with a glory fit for voyagers to eternity.

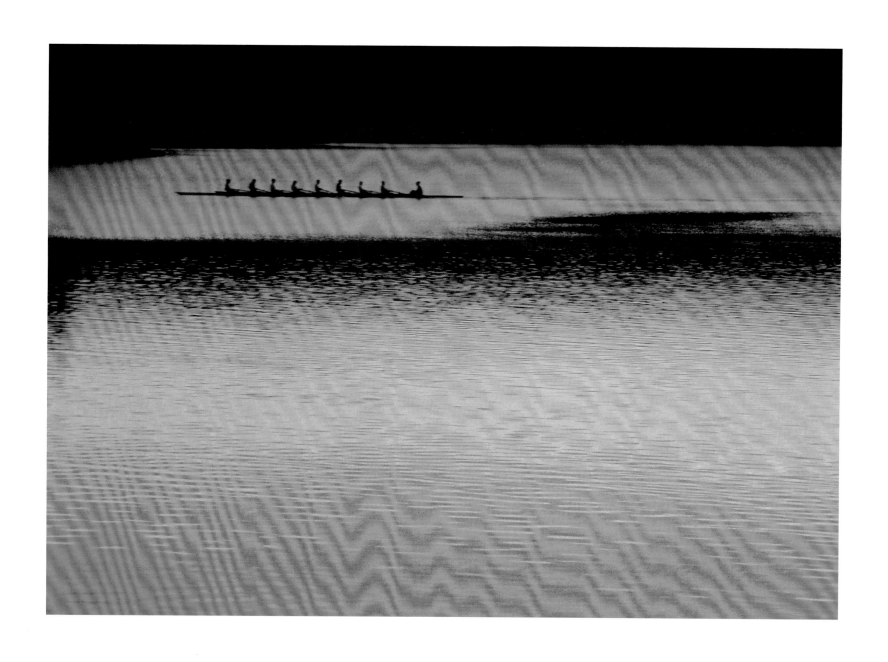

► **CHAPEL PATH BRIDGE**
The path to the chapel hugs the lakeshore and bridges marshy inlets along the way.

► **OLD STEPS IN THE AUTUMN WOODS**
A wayside shrine to John Berchmans—saintly youth, patron of altar
servers at Saint John's—once stood on this knoll. Only the steps remain,
but tints of rose and gold fill the air with glory.

▶
STONE BRIDGE IN WOODS
Some bridges span rivers or bays, others ornament a woodland trail like
this one to Pickerel Point along the shore of Lake Sagatagan. These
weathered stones welcome all who come in peace.

▶

TEKAWITHA STATUE

Tekawitha-Blessed clutches her cross, sign of agony and love. Survivor of the fire at the old Saint Olaf Church, her statue now stands in Collegeville. The trees behind the statue are the oldest planted trees in Minnesota that are not in a town. The Norway spruce and Scotch pine seeds were mailed from Germany and planted after the area was cleared as a result of the 1894 tornado.

▶

WOODS AND WETLANDS SING THE POET'S SONG:

There lives the dearest freshness deep down things;
And though the last lights off the black west went
   Oh, morning, at the brown brink eastward, springs—
Because the Holy Ghost over the bent
   World broods with warm breast and with ah! Bright Wings.
     – Gerard Manley Hopkins, "God's Grandeur"

Adrian Schmitt, O.S.B. (1864-1940), is recognized as the leader in establishing a tradition of forestry at Saint John's. His relatives were governmental foresters in the Black Forest of Baden, Germany. Father Adrian sent them land samples and in turn received both seeds and advice for starting a tree nursery that soon produced fifteen varieties of evergreens planted by the thousands around the campus.

▶

WILDFLOWERS

Fr. Paul Schwietz, a passionate environmentalist and forester, was
responsible for the restoration of the 76-acre prairie and wetlands
at Saint John's. Before he died on May 4, 2000 at the age of 47,
he founded the Saint John's Arboretum (in 1997). The Arboretum
combines the Abbey's 2,500 acres and the university's teaching
skills to create a perfect place for environmental education.

▶

FALL COLORS AND PATTERNS

Big bluestem and Indian grass ripen around a low land island of canary grass.

Father Paul's leadership resulted in the Arboretum's mission:
- Preserve native and historical plant wildlife communities of the Arboretum lands.
- Model practices of sustainable land use.
- Provide opportunites for education and research.
- Make accessible a natural environment that invites spiritual renewal.

▶

WETLANDS AT FOREST EDGE

The majority of the trees on this northern side of the campus were
planted by Ansgar Niess, O.S.B. (1891-1981), during the 1920s and
1930s. The slow and laborious work of planting and raising sensitive
seedlings was a labor of love for Brother Ansgar. At one time he had over
150,000 seedlings in his nursery. In addition to beauty and habitat, the
Arboretum sustainably provides the Abbey wood shop with thousands of
board feet of lumber each year for desks, chairs, tables, and even coffins.

▶
APPLE-PICKING TIME AT COLLEGEVILLE ORCHARD

▶ **EARLY LIGHT AT COLLEGEVILLE ORCHARD
ON FRUIT FARM ROAD**

◄ Open

▶
COLLEGEVILLE ORCHARD STORE
Scherry Beumer patiently and politely tends to her produce.

54

▶

PUMPKINS FOR SALE ON FRUIT FARM ROAD
An eight-second shot with no time to spare as the sun sets over Greg Haeg's
and Megan McNair's home, late October 2003.

◄ *Open*

▶

BACK DOOR TO SAINT JOHN'S
Mother earth puts on the warmth of autumn color and curls up for
winter with the Pflueger farm in the distance.

▶

LATE HARVEST, 2003, ON MEYER'S CENTURY FARM
This is one of several farms adjacent to Saint John's that has been in
the same family for over 100 years.

64

▶

NOSTALGIC FALL DAY ALONG FRUIT FARM ROAD

▶
REMINDER OF A TIME PAST

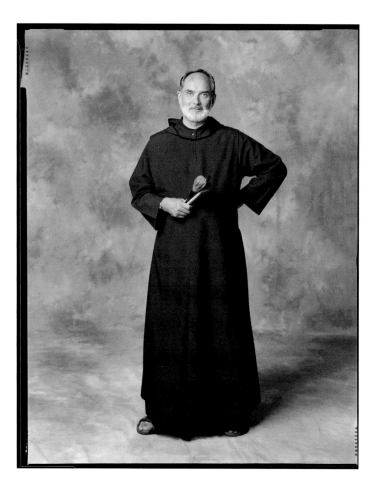

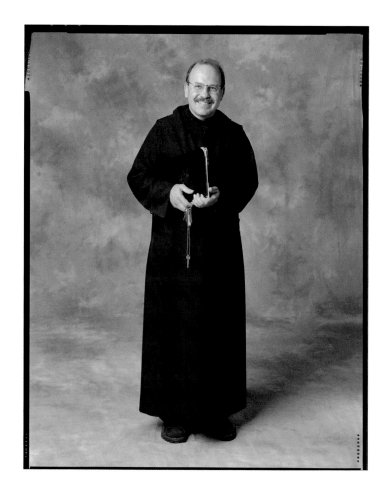

EIGHT MONKS ▶

Left page clockwise:
The Complete Artist
(Jerome Tupa),
The Imperfect Host
(Fran Hoefgen),
The Droll Texan
(J. P. Earls),
The Sober Cyclist
(Dennis Beach)

Right page clockwise:
The Singing Master
(Bart Sayles),
The Numbers Wizard
(Sam Lickteig),
The Prairie Sage
(Paul Schwietz),
The Photographer
of Record
(David Manahan)

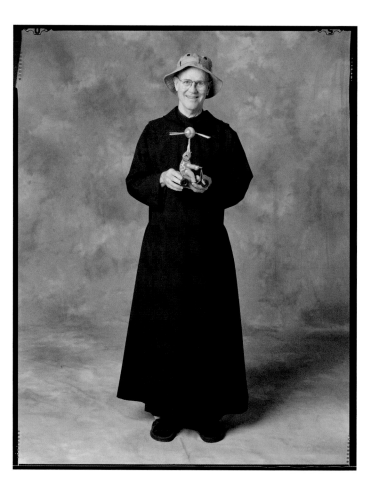

PINESTOCK

Every April, Johnnies and Bennies celebrate the coming of spring with high amplification on what they call "The Island" across Watab from the dorms.

▶
THE JOHNNIE BENCH
Everyone that tries out gets to suit up for home games. The "deep"
bench represents a good percentage of the student body.

◄ *Open*

▶
409TH WIN
John Gagliardi, the winningest college football coach ever with the 409th win—against Bethel on a very cold day in 2003 with 13,500 warming fans.

▶ **JOHN GAGLIARDI AT HOME WITH FAMILY**
John and Peg Gagliardi raised their family of five children from this
home, within walking distance of the SJU football stadium. John is
pictured here one summer afternoon with a few of the grandkids.

MAPLE TREE WITH BAGS

Bags, not buckets, catch the trickling sap from a tapped maple tree deep in the March Abbey woods.

Walter Kieffer, O.S.B., has been involved in sugaring at Saint John's for 40 of the 60 years the Abbey has tapped the sap. Walter indicates that they usually do about 1,200 taps averaging 200-300 gallons of syrup, which is consumed at the Abbey or given to friends of the Abbey.

TRACTOR AT SUGAR SHACK
At the sugar shack the tractor-drawn sap tanker perches on a knoll covered with winter grasses.

▶

THREE MONKS WITH JUGS OF SYRUP
A trio of maple-syrup cooks settle for payment in kind and head back to
the cloister at the end of the day.

▶

MASTER POTTER RICHARD BRESNAHAN
Bresnahan bas been an artist-in-residence at Saint John's since 1979.
Just prior to that time, he earned the title of master potter by apprenticing
3-1/2 years with Nakazato Takashi, a thirteenth-generation Japanese potter.
Bresnahan, unlike most American Potters, uses local clay and locally
derived glazes to give his work a distinctive Saint John's pottery look.

▶
THE OLD KILN
This may have been Richard Bresnahan's last burn before the old
Takigame kiln was dismantled, making way for Sexton Commons. A new
kiln, the Johanna Kiln, named in honor of Richard's mentor, Sister
Johanna Beeker, was finished by Bresnahan in October, 1994 after two
years of planning and construction. It is the largest wood burning kiln
in North America.

▶

SWAYED PINE FEST
Each spring musicians compete for the hearts of judges and fans while crafts
and food are offered during the daylong event on the college campus.

▶

FATHER GALL
Father Gall puts on his hat to go for a walk and decides to sit for a while
in the sun.

▶

SINGERS IN CHURCH

"All you hosts of the Lord, bless the Lord!" These tenors are on call at the firehouse if the emergency beepers on their belts sound. They blend their work as they blend their voices against the honeycomb backdrop of the great north wall of the church.

▶ **JOE O'CONNELL'S PASSION AND PROFESSION**
Joe O'Connell in his final days, completing his labor of love in limestone
for Christ the King Catholic Community in Las Vegas, 4-1/2 years in the
making.

▶

O'CONNELL HOUSE FRONT DOOR
"Let me live in a house by the side of the road and be a friend to man"
might have been the inscription over Joe and Jody O'Connell's
Collegeville door. Sunlight and leaves of pale gold say it without words.

BROTHER PLACID AND WHITE HORSE
Artist from Montana, Brother Placid, and his white horse that will go anywhere in imagination.

▶

MONKS IN FRONT OF GARDEN HOUSE
A summer afternoon at the Garden House. It is the season of short
shadows and long days. Tolerant gardeners rest in the sun, unhurried
in the time of growing, God's time.

▶

ROOT CELLAR
Crates of carrots and onions and 30-gallon crocks of sauerkraut
are kept cool in the garden root cellar to grace the winter table with
no-nonsense meals for hungry boys and their teachers.

▶
OLD WATER TOWER DOOR
The old 1890 water tower was an early abbey structure. In his history, Hilary refers to its architecture as akin to a medieval keep positioned on a high point on the abbey property so that it could be used as a celestial observation point. The water tower is still being used as a reservoir for the ground watering system.

▶
GREAT HALL
In the '60s the dominant twin towers of the old Abbey Church gave
way to the massive bell banner of the new abbey church just yards away.
The result was a towerless Great Hall with magnificent wood, stained glass,
and ceiling paintings. The open space now is a perfect reception area.

THE GREAT HALL

▶ **AUTUMN IVY IN COURTYARD**
In the monastery courtyard burnished ivy makes the cold corridor warmer outdoors than it ever was indoors.

▶
QUAD GABLES IN THE RAIN
Not the rooftops of Paris, but the gables and chimneys of Abbot Alexius
Edelbrock's 1886 Quadrangle on a rainy day—before the wooden shingles
and facing were replaced with weathered copper for the next century.
Generations of preps and college students slept in open dorms behind
these windows.

THE QUAD AND COMPANY
The old brick buildings hunker down close to the ground, earth-rooted
beneath a painter's sky: clouds, light, and motion.

► **CLASSROOM WINDOWS AND DESKS**
A Quad classroom as students saw it for a hundred years: plain plaster walls, high energy-inefficient windows, sizzling radiator, a jumble of desk chairs where sentences could be parsed or Latin verbs conjugated or dates matched with names of presidents in American history.

▶

LOWER CHAPEL ENTRANCE
A modest entrance of homemade brick covers six steps leading down
to the lower chapel of the 1882 church. Here the brothers prayed, the
fathers said their masses, and zealous parishioners satisfied their Sunday
obligation at 5:30 a.m. before other business could intervene.

▶

ABBEY CHURCH CORNERSTONE

Abbot Baldwin Dworshak had great courage and foresight to adopt
architect Marcel Breuer's grand designs for a one-hundred-year plan
to restructure the entire campus with the new Abbey Church as its
centerpiece. The plan was abandoned in 1979 when seventeen historic
buildings were accepted into the national register. The church and a
few other Breuer-influenced structures are a stark contrast to the old
brick buildings (the Quad in the six previous images), but seem to
coexist nicely, old and permanent, and new and permanent.

   The new (1961) Abbey Church is clearly an architectural feat. This is
a structure that as a photographer you know that there are great images
that can be captured here but just how to do it is another story. Much
thought and effort went into our interpretation of what "worked."

▶
BELIE OF THE BANNER

"This is the house of God and the gate of heaven." This great arch dwarfs and dignifies processions that pass beneath it: bishops, monks, faculties, and students. On Saturday afternoons wedding parties linger beneath it. Under its broad reach the monks form a great circle to embrace their newly vowed brothers on the feast of Benedict.

FLAP COVER: A rare view of the banner with hoarfrost.

 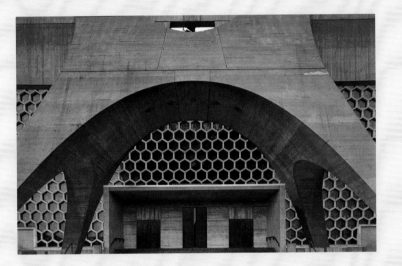

◀ Open

▶
VIEW FROM EAST OF ABBEY CHURCH
The play of light and shadow vindicate architect Marcel Breuer's
audacious geometry.

▶

SLICE OF NORTH WALL OF ABBEY CHURCH

To capture on film the free support expanse of the Abbey Church balcony is
almost impossible. Tons of concrete went into the ground to counterbalance
the unsupported front of the balcony. This is one of Breuer's legacies.

◄ *Open*

▶
STAINED GLASS. WINDOW OF OPPORTUNITY.
This image is dedicated to the present Abbot, Abbot John Klassen for his courage to deal with the data on sexual abuse at Saint John's. And to A. W. Richard Sipe, brother and uncle of the photographers, for his dedication and passion in defending the harmed, educating the willing, and assisting in reform.

MIKE SIPE has spent much of his life in the Collegeville area, and is a graduate of Saint John's prep school and Saint John's University. He is a mid- and large-format photography enthusiast. He became interested in photography in 1969 when his dad gave him $100 to buy a camera in Germany while stationed there in the Army. Mike had little time for photography during the '70s—he and his wife Patty were raising their two children, and he was working as a CPA in St. Cloud. Minnesota. He got inspired about photography again in the mid-1980s, after attending a workshop with the environmental photographer Craig Blacklock. Mike is currently a CFP (Certified Financial Planner) and CPA and is the majority owner of AIS Planning, a life wealth planning practice in St. Cloud. He is trying to practice the life balance he preaches at work by spending more time on his photography.

MICHAEL SIPE grew up in St. Cloud Minnesota and attended Saint John's Prep School and Saint John's University from 1984-1992 graduating with a BA in Sociology and German. He began photography at an early age, worked for camera stores during summer breaks, and later assisted professional photographers until becoming one himself. He works out of his studio in beautiful Burlington, Vermont, and at present feels that his best work is the environmental portrait. He is truly inspired by his 2 1/2 year old daughter Avi Mae, who is completely awake even in her sleep.

HILARY THIMMESH, O.S.B., comes from Osakis, Minnesota, where he was born in 1928. A graduate of Saint John's University with a doctorate in English from Cornell University, he has taught at Saint John's since 1963 and served in several administrative positions, including the presidency of the University from 1982 to 1991. He is a priest, a would-be poet, and an all-seasons hiker in the woods and ways of Collegeville.

ACKNOWLEDGMENTS

It has been well over ten years since this book was first contemplated and there are many people to thank who helped us along the way.

We would like to thank Patty (wife and Mom), for her consistent encouragement, honesty, and patience. Thanks also to Bridget (daughter and sister) for her words of support. And Avi Mae (granddaughter and daughter) for being. To Michael's old friend Ben Johnson for illuminating Michael's career path.

This is our first photography fine art publication. Like most firsts, the learning curve is steep. Thank you to the following people for their training and patience: Bill Harvey—book design; Kathy, Rose, and Jess at Digital Engine—prepress; and Julie Stillman—editor.

Thank you to Hilary for staying with *Collegeville* so long, and for his very informative and interesting history of the Abbey. Thanks also to Tom Kroll, director of Saint John's Arboretum, for his research and information editing.

Printed and bound in China by Palace Press Int'l.

Prepress by Digital Engine
Edited by Julie Stillman
Production assistance by Sylvie Vidrine
Book design by Bill Harvey

ISBN 0-976836I-0-6